- Facing the Darkness -

B KAY MACKLE

First published in Far North Queensland, 2025 by Bowerbird Publishing

© 2025 B. Kay Mackle

The moral rights of the author have been asserted. All rights reserved. Except as permitted under the Australian Copyright Act 1968 (for example, a fair dealing for the purposes of study, research, criticism or review), no part of this book may be reproduced, stored in a retrieval system, communicated or transmitted in any form or by any means without prior written permission. All enquiries should be made to the author.

ISBN 978 1 7637660 5 1 (paperback)
ISBN 978 1 7637660 6 8 (ebook)

The Grey Wolf
Facing the Darkness
B. Kay Mackle

First edition: 2025

Edited by: Crystal Leonardi, Bowerbird Publishing
Interior & Cover Design by: Crystal Leonardi, Bowerbird Publishing

Distributed by Bowerbird Publishing
Available in National Library of Australia

Disclaimer: The material in this publication is of the nature of general comment only, and does not represent professional advice. It is not intended to provide specific guidance for particular circumstances and it should not be relied on as the basis of any decision to take action or not take action on any matter which it covers. Readers should obtain professional advice where appropriate, before making any such decision. To the maximum extent permitted by law, the author and publisher disclaim all responsibility and liability to any person, arising directly or indirectly from any person taking or not taking action based on the information in this publication.

Bowerbird Publishing
Julatten, Queensland, Australia
www.crystalleonardi.com

For family, with thoughts of J. Mackle.
In memory of David Voltz.

I was inspired to write about the subject of mental health by my GP.

Bringing mental dialogue to mind,
recalling truth,
remembering the dark days.

A passage in time,
a doorway of regret,
that is hard to forget.

There has been a window of support,
with an energy source of connection.
Which now allows in the light of love and kindness
to brighten each new day.

INTRODUCTION

Words you may have heard.
Words you may have said.
It's all in your head.
What's the matter with you?
There is nothing wrong with you.
What have you done all day?
You are lazy.
You are useless.
You are a waste of space.
No space for you here.
Get out of bed.
Get out of that chair.
Get up. Get out. Get a job.
Get off that device.
Stop watching TV.
Get on with your life.
No one will want you how you are.
Go clean yourself up.
Go outside.
I don't know what to do for you.
Go and get someone else's advice.
Please.
Go read a book.

THE SPACE IN BETWEEN

The spaceship has been on a universal tracking mission
in the solar system.

It circles the universe in outer space, to find a place,
an opportunity to land on Earth.

This craft blots out the sunshine.
It has been in waiting, lingering overhead, looking down from
space, looking for an open break to enter,
seeking a window of opportunity.

Ship X drifts around at intervals until the controller is asleep.
It transports Grey Wolf, Black Wolf, and Shadow
to the Earth Plane.

Ship X has landed.

The commander and his constant companions have arrived.

I know it. I remember it. I sense it.

I feel its presence. I cannot see it.

It is not alien to me.

I know the ship is hovering above my bed.

I hear it in my head.

I can't find the off switch in the dark.

This spaceship has visited me many times.

I have named it 'X' for anXiety.

When the large door opens the visitors arrive,
bringing who I don't want or need in my life;
the demons have turned up again.

Grey Wolf, Black Wolf, and Shadow.
I have named them Flicker, Dangerfield and Shade.

These are the ones to blame for my pain,
my cloudy days and unclear thoughts.

Flicker, Dangerfield and Shade
have the power to get into my brain.

I don't want visitors that arrive uninvited.
I don't want anyone knocking on my door.
I don't want a cup of tea.

Not today.
Not tomorrow or any other day.

Day and night, I hold on tight to my head,
feeling that dreadful sense of losing control.
The stress is too much to bear.
I could possibly lose my hair.
My school work,
my work load has put too much pressure on me.

These three wolves that follow me can change my behaviour
and my train of thought at will.

I feel like I am losing control and struggling with a constant
state of uneasiness.
Stress overwhelms me.
What am I to address?
Trauma has imprinted itself in my being.

In a grip of fear, I confess, to safe guard my sanity.

I decide to call a friend, they don't have time to listen.
This makes me feel weak, silly and pathetic.
I decide to call the doctor. Why?
I am not sick. I am not dying.
No appointment available today anyway.
Get on with it, I say.

I can't, the wheels are spinning.
The fear is returning.
One thing after another.
I can't go out, I am afraid.
What's that noise?
This is no joke.

I can't bring myself to go for a walk.
The path is too narrow.
I might see someone I know.
They might recognise my pattern of behaviour.
They might think I am weird.

I could get hit by a bike or a flying bird.
I can't drive the car. I might lose my direction.
I will probably get lost.
I don't have the ability to read a map. I could lose my way.
I definitely can't drive at night; the lights are too bright.

I can't bring myself to go to the shops,
there will be too many people around.
I don't want to speak to anyone, I might cry.
Get over it! At least try.

Flicker fuels my fears.
This makes my body start to shiver and shake.

I don't want to eat. There is poison in the wheat.
What do I drink? Everything is bad for you, even the water.

Fish are drowning in a sea of rubbish.
Don't eat meat!
Don't eat dairy!
Your cholesterol is too high!
Chemicals are in our food supply.

Pollution in the air I breathe.
Plastic breaking up. Bring your own cup.

Unrest in foreign countries. War is imminent in the future.
There is no future!?

Money, it's all about money.
What about the bees and the trees!
No more flowers! No more seeds! No honey!
No life.

What's up? you hear.
You don't look happy.
For goodness' sake smile.

Are you OK?
Let's do coffee.
Do you want to talk about it?
What is troubling you?

I have nothing to say.
I don't want to explain the X,
Flicker, Dangerfield or Shade.
No one understands my fears.
They will think I am crazy.

I will be fine.
It will just take time.
Good day or bad day,
I manage on my own.

I have the phone.
I turn off the phone.
Alone, isolated, dehydrated.
When did you start grinding your teeth?

Flicker is getting too close for comfort.
Dangerfield and Shade follow my every move.
I need to get ahead of them and stop my thinking.

I think of a hobby.
What could I possibly do?
I have no interest in anything new.
I am in my head. Full stop.
Don't you understand!
The switch is on night and day.

I am tired all of the time. I cannot sleep.
I am testing all that I eat.
I am losing weight from the pressure of it all.
Life is not what it is cracked up to be.
I don't like me.

I wish I could crack open my skull and drag out the nasty, the negative, the upsetting and unwanted thoughts.
This is becoming serious.
I can't handle it.
I can't get over it.

Why so sad?
Why so glum?
I start chewing my gum.
I bite my lip.

I know I should go for a walk.
How long? How far? My feet hurt.
One excuse after another. I am sensitive.
The sun will burn.
It might get too hot.
It might rain. It might get cold.
Who knows the weather?

Just suppose!?
Flicker fades away and Dangerfield and Shade go missing!
I could go to the beach!
I could go for a swim!
I can't swim.

Flicker might go out in the water.
Dangerfield and Shade might run behind and play follow the
leader, then take one step further
into the deep fathoms and drown.
Forget that!
Dogs can paddle.
I could. I should.
I might be alright, if I address all my obstacles,
my worries and my fears.

I have cried enough tears.
I have had nightmares for years.

I need to talk it through.
If I face up to Flicker, Dangerfield and Shade,
they may fade away.
They could possibly disappear.
I will demand they leave me alone.
I wonder if that will work?

I can't find the slow down, easy fix,
exit or stop buttons in my mind to test a reaction.
I need to talk to someone that understands.
I need to rest my mental body.
I know I need to exercise my physical body.
But still I resist.

I know I am not alone.
I know there are others suffering the same emotions.
Where can we get help?
Hospital for observation?
Not for me. It might be ok for you.

I don't want to be locked up analysed, judged or labelled.
I want to be free, happy and confident.
I want joy, love and peace.

We all could get on a cruise ship and sail away.
We all could get of an aeroplane and fly away.
But I know Flicker, Dangerfield and Shade
will follow us wherever we go.
There will always be a thought in the mind
that will keep them there.

Sometimes hiding, sometimes quiet,
but they are a constant presence and noise
in the back of the mind.
They weigh me down, and they tie me down.

I need to get out.
I decide to go it alone.
My confidence grows.

Step up! Step out!
Without warning, there is a pain in my chest.
My heart is pounding.
Is it a heart attack?
I can't catch my breath.

Am I going to die?
There are lights flashing.
I am sweating.
I feel dizzy and nauseous.
Am I going to pass out in the street?
A panic attack!
I need to go back in where I feel safe.
Lock the door!

Help is needed.
I feel the friction.
Am I starting an addiction?

There is no speedy recovery.
It will take time and effort.
I know, I understand.
I see the possibilities.
I take one step.
As I am.

Be prepared!
Hey, relax and quiet the mind.
Be aware of the breath.
Work and play, dance and sing, paint or draw.
Get your hands dirty. Start a garden.
Repair in fresh clean air.

Still the mind.
Eat organic.

Ring until you find a friend, a medical practitioner, therapist,
healer or spiritualist that you trust and most definitely need.
Meditation might be your medicine.

Even if all you require is a listening ear, someone to listen,
someone to understand, someone who believes your suffering.
There is no shame in taking advice.

Natural therapies may be recommended.
It might comfort the spirit and the soul.
There is no shame in taking medication from a qualified GP.
It may be necessary to alter a chemical imbalance.

Recognise unrest has come from a sequence of events.
At times a spiritual practitioner or a person connected to a church might be a calling you are willing to explore.

There is help available.
There are organisations with quality information.
Counsellors, Lifeline, Beyondblue, The Black dog Institute,
Head Space, Suicide prevention, to name a few.
Look for them in your area.
Write down their numbers in case of emergency.

When the alien Ship X, the past, brings the darkness,
trouble and distress, clouds make the present foggy,
heavy and dull, allowing anxiety to arise.

This is a timely reminder to move forward to command release.

Look to the light of a new day on this passage way of hope.
It is a reminder, a time to pause, breathe, relax,
become calm and reset.

Take a break from the mind, meditate into a space of the heart.
Flow with the river of time, to happier moments,
minutes and hours to recover the now days.

If you can't find a way to tame Flicker (anxiety),
depression will take control.
Now is the time to face that Black Wolf Dog and Shadow.
Turn around, look that Wolf Dog in the eye.
Cast the shadow aside.

Train Black Wolf to sit by your side,
to stay, to go away on command.

Tell them to both fetch the stick and don't come back.
Throw it far away, over a cliff.
Watch and observe as they both disappear
from your mind and your sight.
Be prepared to let them go.

Replace this vision with one of calm, courage and conviction.
Walk a new light path of confidence.

Please don't go down the dark narrow road to suicide.
Decide to live.
Decide to forgive.
Decide to accept the consequences of living
and dying in one lifetime.

Look now to a better day, a brighter day and night.

Change is constant.
Find a new way to picture a light switch that can be
turned ON or OFF at will.
Imagine and allow a White Wolf to appear as a protector,
a guide and a friend.
Let's call this new companion 'Flow'.

Snuggle up and let's get a good night's sleep.

How to identify anxiety.
Can't look in the mirror.
Nothing positive to say.

How to recognise depression.
Can't get out of bed.
Why bother getting dressed?

Close the door. Pull down the blinds.
Needing darkness. Sensing withdrawal.

This behaviour leads to not wanting to be here.
Raining every day and night. When will it clear?

Pray for a better day, one of sunshine and light.

The shadow does not lift.
A dark day exists.
Even the ducks look sad.

I have made up my mind.
I decide.
I am going to be with Mum and Dad.

Life is not worth living as I am.
Sorry, the endless chronic pain is too much to bear any longer.
I agonise over my decision.
My prospects are not good.
The waiting game is over.
I love you so much.
Suicide.

In death comes release.
Peace.

AUTHOR'S NOTE

The source of early childhood trauma, verbal or physical abuse, controlled actions, dominance, debilitating body injury, plus grief and loss, can all bring on low self-esteem, and low self-worth issues. These can be triggers, that bring about sadness, low energy and withdrawal.

As a result, these emotions cause the prospect of self-harm to the body, loss of spirit, plus damage to the soul, resulting in loss of faith.

What follows is sadness, worry, anxiety and fear of living. Consequently, these actions have the ability to bring on depression, with the thought that there is no hope for the future.

Restoring energy requires patience, in addition to lots of effort.

A cry for help is required/desired to bring back self-belief, self-control, courage, strength and confidence. To live one's own life. Allow a positive result with good intentions and a grateful heart. Acceptance and forgiveness enable release. As I release and let go, I trust. My conscience is clear. My faith is restored.

My soul speaks. I accept and feel the miracles of life. I let love flow and onward/forward I go, guided by the light. I allow myself to be rich in spirit and rich in receiving.

I live in creative harmony with all that is.

Life is a miracle. Life has a purpose. Born to be free. My soul gives and receives universal love. Let us not fall from grace. Life is not a race it is a learning opportunity. A cycle of realisation.

AFFIRMATION

Today, I choose to find joy in the little things.
Not stress over what I cannot control.
Be kind, not just to others, but to myself.
To stay hopeful, not hopeless.
I choose to follow my heart, not my head,
nor the noise around me.

I do one thing just for me every day,
because I am worth it.
I value myself, my life, my light.

I do my best.
I am enough.
I am.

ABOUT THE AUTHOR

B. Kay Mackle is passionate about her soul mission. With courage and a hopeful exploration of mental health, Kay offers her readers a poetic, powerful narrative that will resonate deeply with anyone who has experienced the pain of anxiety, depression, or trauma.

For those seeking understanding, support, or simply a reminder that they are not alone in their struggles, Kay's publications are a warm companion. The heart of the writing is clear: healing is possible, and we can find peace, even in the spaces in between.

OTHER TITLES BY B. KAY MACKLE

~ Master Forest Wizard

~ Time to Help Bundy Blue

~ The Power of Three: Darkness to Light

~ The Purpose of Three: In a Garden of Choice

~ The Broken Branch Grows: Poeticized Writings in Verse

~ Stepping Stones: Walk the Path

Contact author B Kay Mackle at kaym@internode.on.net

FROM THE PUBLISHER

In 'The Grey Wolf', B Kay Mackle offers an intimate look into the struggles of the mind, presenting the everyday challenges of living with mental health issues.

The book is structured as a journey—a journey not only through the author's personal experiences but also a universal one that many readers will see mirrored in their own lives. Kay uses metaphors like the spaceship 'Ship X' and characters such as Grey Wolf, Black Wolf, and Shadow to personify anxiety and its destructive power.

The Grey Wolf's message is to reclaim agency over one's mind through self-compassion, connection, and patience. Kay gently urges readers to face their fears, challenge negative thoughts, and embrace their own resilience. With warmth, empathy, and a focus on personal empowerment, The Grey Wolf is a beautiful, moving reflection on the journey from despair to hope.

I wish Kay all the very best in her continued journey through authorship and congratulate her on another exceptional publication.

Crystal Leonardi
Bowerbird Publishing
www.crystalleonardi.com

www.ingramcontent.com/pod-product-compliance
Lightning Source LLC
Chambersburg PA
CBHW072138070526
44585CB00016B/1733